Feelings

REGLA TERESA DOMINGUEZ

NEWMAN SPRINGS PUBLISHING
320 Broad Street
Red Bank, NJ 07701

First originally published by Newman
Springs Publishing 2021

ISBN 978-1-63692-769-5 (Paperback)
ISBN 978-1-63692-770-1 (Digital)

Printed in the United States of America

Collaborators' data

Cover: José Luis Colina Rodríguez—Sotheby´s New York

Correction: Idalmi Díaz Rivas—EBENEZER Producciones Cuba

General Coordinator and Edition: Gelacio Alberto Dominguez Prieto—EBENEZER Producciones Cuba

Translation: Pedro Valois Dominguez—PhD in Education. CICEP, Mexico.

This small book of verses is specially dedicated to the people who have impacted my life and who have developed in me who I am today—people I have loved, I keep loving, and I will love unconditionally and from whom I have always received support.

To my son, my parents, my brothers, but especially to my beloved husband, for the beautiful love that we lived, which was intercepted by his departure, this is a written revelation, a release of relief at his absence.

This work is dedicated to our love and the love to our son.

May the Lord reward your work, and let your reward
be fulfilled from the Lord God of Israel, under
whose wings you have come to take refuge.

—Ruth 2:12

Contents

Foreword

As poetry, *Feelings* ties its essence and style in the strength of a personality and a vital experience. From here, it's a unifying thread and an exclusive seal in the emotional skein of a soul capable of going out to the outside world in precise words.

Because, far from a purely emotional sentimentality, each poem in the book contains and spills feelings in the form of conviction. It is not about making people cry or recreating emotions on the surface. Complicity with the reader is born from universal reactions to pain, love, impotence, despair, and also hope.

Beyond nostalgia and beyond loneliness, there remains a tribute, a kind of recognition through life toward unforgettable beings, those who genetically and spiritually design the close relationships of every human being.

However, the existentialist or philosophical tone does not prevail. On the contrary, the verses translate concrete experiences. As you read, clear, capsulelike images emerge—the warmth of a look, the smell or the physique of a person reborn, or the dream that overcomes thought. But described in simple terms, in a kind of inner monologue, which explains itself, it asks and answers itself while showing the meaning of a feeling objectively.

Therefore, the greater or lesser length of a verse does not clash. The ideas flow like a totally natural conversation, surprising by turning what is thought into a poem, sometimes, into an unapproachable rush of daily reflection. Above all, the accuracy of the image and the idea matters even if creative licenses are required to achieve this.

The intimate tone, which marks the first person in many of the texts, justifies the stylistic freedom of the verses without being tied to strict meter or conventional rhyme. However, the rhythm beats with the force of the heart within the verses or successive lines, like bursts that cannot be stopped, only in signs that mark the air and the tone above the grammar.

Anaphora, enumeration, and contrast of phrases and ideas identify, embellish, and link the poems, diverse as the inspiration itself and the events of reality.

The metaphor recurs with associative spontaneity and not out of sheer aestheticism, as much as the closings as a sentence, a precise synthesis of the feeling and the inspiring motive.

Difficult are classifications in a text as authentic as it is antiformal. The themes of wide frequency oscillate from the inner revelation to the declaration of principles and the social position as an implicit denunciation.

Reaffirm and not just remember. Revive instead of dying or letting the memory die. Transform emotion into creation. Define this first work without transcendentalism but overflowing with shared experience in the future of one and many—so many—people.

Idalmi Diaz Rivas

Acknowledgments

I thank all the people who helped me make this little dream come true.

To my brother, for the collaboration and connection with the visual artist in charge of the cover of the book, who knew how to show in that image the eccentricity of the naked soul in a very proper way to reflect the interior of my feelings—loneliness, fear, nostalgia, pain, love, helplessness, frustrations, and fulfillment—during a stage of my life which defined the origin of this small book of verses, expelling all manifestations of human exhaustion to the outside to leave only a naked body of emotions.

Absurd

From my balcony, I watch
the sleeping sky;
it seems his eyes are closing
because evening is falling,
and the arrogant fragrance of this disturbing night
makes it clear that the day is gone.

I am sad to see the empathy of the night
knowing that I will spend hours awake,
longing for the rising day
which will take long to arrive
if I don't close my eyes.
And already tired of looking at the moon
that from my window
says good night to me,
I fall in the arms of Morpheus
just like an empress.

When You Close Your Eyes

When you close your eyes
the door was closed to my hope;
the clock stopped at 2:56 p.m.;
I remember it started to rain nonstop.
It seems that even heaven was crying for your loss;
everything became confusing and dark;
a new stage was beginning for me.

When you close your eyes
for me, it was a challenge to life
looking at the rest of humanity
With hurt eyes, full of tears.
The illusion of love was extinguished;
a new person arose in me
that it would take time to get to know each other.

When you close your eyes
the need for you is indescribable.
A challenge to life was declared;
began a virtual and spiritual communication between us
to be able to subsist, to overcome the obstacles that would
    come,
to be able to offer a strong arm to my son,
to be the support to the rest of the family.
But believe me, my dear, that there is a hope of seeing us
    again
when I close my eyes.

At Birth

For your dad, you represent
a new figure
that would entail love,
responsibility, time,
dedication, example.

For your mom, you represent
a continuity of a being that should love, feed, care, and watch
because he grew up healthy and strong.

For both of us, you represent
a sweet and attractive fruit that, when ripe,
it would be served to society.
You represent a very valuable jewel
that would be polished and protected at all costs
to make it shine outside in due course.

You represent a symbol
that would seal a living, growing, and burning love
that would last even further
of losing your breath.

Our son—our fruit, jewel, and symbol
you represent so much to us
that you are the reason for our deeds,
our dreams, our challenges,
our triumphs, our lives.

Love

Love is to undress the soul;
it is revealing yourself to the possible and the impossible;
it is to win;
it is starting and reaching the goal; it is giving everything,
with or without risks,
even without rewards.

Love, it is beautiful to live it,
because it transforms you,
makes you show all the emotions:
joy, jealousy, sadness, anger, pleasure, pain...
And it transports you to the unknown,
to another dimension;
you don't care if you know it or not.
Makes you strong,
makes you weak,
and commits you to give everything of yourself,
without intending it.

Loving is beautiful;
it is a divine feeling.
With love, you can create a human being,
a better world,
and live fully.

Love in Darkness

Screaming love,
love in silence,
love that hurts,
love that pours out love,
love that provides energy,
values, dreams, desires, challenges, confidence,
tenderness, security, beliefs, roots.

Love that grows
like mustard tree
immense in branches and
leafy in fruits.

Love that unleashes love
to the neighbor, to yours, to strangers, enemies, and friends.

Love that is transmitted as
electric current flow
like blood
circulating through the veins.

Love that is feared,
because there is a lot of love.
Love of decades,
of generations, of the future.

Love of landscapes,
of memories,
of books, of smells.
Love without measures, without restrictions,
out of control.
Only that excessive love throbbing for you,
my love in me.

To My God

Someone asked me one day,
"And why don't you write to God?"
Hmm, good question!
To my God,
I speak to Him daily.
Isn't it God who sustains me?
He knows everything about me.
With my God, I have talks at different times of the day.
He is not bored with me,
does not stop answering me
nor ignore my calls.
Always attentive to hear my prayers,
my compliments, my songs, my prayers…
He is constant.
He is patient.
God is the light on the way.
That is why we must go to Him
in search of guidance, wisdom, understanding…
Without His company, we can get lost.
He is love and peace.
Not always ready to answer when I cry out to Him,
but it's amazing how it makes me understand,
justify, and accept it when He is silent or when He answers me
in a different way than I expect.
He knows everything about me
even when it hasn't happened.
I don't need to write to Him.
He is up-to-date with me and knows how much He means
    in my life.

Human brothers have to remind ourselves
how much we love each other,
how much we do for each other.
He does not...He is in ourselves, our shadow,
our question, our answer,
the air, the water, the food that sustains us.
It is our light, our soon shelter.
It is all in one. It's God!
He doesn't need me to write to Him. I sing to Him.
He likes me to talk to Him more.

Through My Eyes

I see the full moon in your eyes,
the Christmas of your smile,
the fan of your hands
that move
with mechanical wisdom of expert maturity.
I breathe in the fragrance of your sweat
accompanied by the memory of your years.

Through my eyes,
I want to remember your simplicity,
the murmur of your lips,
battered by time but still standing as two parallel lines,
from which gushes of love sprout
tenderness and hope.

Loving and remembering you is present and future.
It's having you here, watching you.
You are my solid rock and, at the same time, my soft velvet
        where my spirit rests.
You have been the central idea in the paragraph of my life,
for which I have ruled myself in the passage of time.
It is you, Mother, through my eyes.

Troubled

Silence, murmurs, screams
inside my lips
inside me, troubled.

Ideas, purposes, goals
inside my thoughts
inside me, troubled.

Unfinished, confusing actions
vague, insecure
inside me, troubled.

And I wonder: is it possible to shred this trouble
which immerses me in an immense sea of worries
and drowns the spirit
to keep myself alive?
And then floating in this troublesome trouble
that suddenly ceases, striking
an immense wall of faith and future hope
that strengthens my lips, my ideas, my actions.

Absence

Sweat, the outside of the walls,
by the morning dew.
Early, the bird sings,
to show your presence.
The tired rose fades,
the air carries away the dirty and brings dust...
You are not.
They've all gone,
and I'm still breathing,
suffering from the pain of not seeing you,
of justified indifference,
of the love of my entrails,
of fear, of circumstances.
Even so, the city still stands:
the houses, the cars, the people, the walls,
the roses, the dust, my son, your absence, and me.

I Believe

I believe in the sunset
I believe in the smile of a child
I believe in the message of good preaching
I believe in alternatives, in options
and in good vibes
I believe in the determination of the human being
I believe in personal values
I believe in miracles and divine grace
I believe in the power of prayer
I believe in family
I believe in the love of my husband
I believe in my son's values
I believe in my spiritual strength
And for all this, I think we can dream and idealize dreams
and achieve them anywhere in the world
wherever we are.

Kid

I heard about a little boy
that, at his early age,
has made wonders;
he climbed in the iron bars,
spinning like a top,
stretchy and bold;
and he did not care about the danger.
It turned out that, that little boy,
modest and very polite,
had very well kept in his heart
a God.
And with his ability, faith, and gift,
he went to another city
and won an award.
As a member of a
sport-winning team,
this year,
he was recognized
because in the bar, as well as in
in jumping or in the parallels,
he beats everyone.

I tell you that this skinny boy,
with defined muscles and small stature,
was called "the star child"
by his classmates
because there was a desire in him
to share and help the most in need,
and that is added to
his bearing and his behavior.

We can expect from him
an outstanding athlete
that will travel the world
and who will insist
on breaking records and achieving triumphs.

—Dedicated to my nephew Josué

Inside of Me

Inside of me,
a bunch of emotions,
a tragic sadness,
a precipice of tears,
an abyss of loneliness,
an unbridled desire to love you.
A challenge to this feeling
of not accepting to lose you.

Since You Are Not

Each projection is black and white
as if the colors of everything around me
would have disappeared.
Every joy is a tasteless
every laugh is a grimace
every day is a rehearsal
each work is mechanical
every step of walking is forced.
Only crying, only sighing
only loneliness is with me
since you are not.

Devoid

I slowly remove the anger
for your absence.
Slowly I let go of the anguish, the despair, and the uncertainty
that I will not see you again.
Softly and still with tears in my eyes,
I am devoid of emotions.

I stay still for a moment and internalize
that there will be no more your kisses, your hugs,
your deep gaze that undressed
my body and my mind,
your common sense to all our things,
your laugh, which was contagious and spread to others.

Still in no rush and stripped of emotions,
I try to cover my pain with the love of our son,
with the love that we had,
with faith and hope
that one day we will meet again.

Give Me Back

Eight years have passed,
and I see no solution.
Please give me back my missing arm
to hold me,
my right leg missing
to go to faraway places without thinking about the danger.
My heart still bleeds;
make this hemorrhage stop.
My cracked eyes,
because they are dry from crying,
they ask to smile again
and see life with enlightened eyes
full of dreams again.
Give me back
my safe steps, where to go,
because they don't want to walk alone;
they ask for company.
And what can I do with my words
that only listen to my echo
as a monologue,
who are crying out with whom to talk.
Give me back
who was I before you left
because I've lost my way.
You taught me a lot about life:
how to move forward and be the first but not
how to do if I'm the last.

She

She walks lightly.
It seems that the load that she carries
did not weigh her down.
She smiles, and it isn't an elaborate grin;
it is a genuine smile.
She tells you about her projects determined and decided.
But God knows her fears, her hesitations…
because He is her partner and witness
in the constant talks of the day.

She gives encouragement to others
if they need it.
But she is trapped in her judgment, in her grief…
Ready to supply her peers
but slow and doubtful
to supply herself.

She is passionate and dedicated in everything she does.
She passionately loved
and was loved in the same way.
She found her other half,
her compatible horoscope,
her chemistry in adventures and dreams.
But she doubts that an equal opportunity will appear.
Tenacity and courage are her cover,
but in her inner notebook,
many contradictions, disagreements, doubts, fears…
And you have to know her because she is unique.
It is her, and she is me.

Escape

Who has not ever felt trapped?
In the mosquito net of life's problems
where his heart beats like a "bembé drum"
without finding a way out.
And it's just suffocation
as a solution to the unknown which leads
you to the adventure of triumph.

Countries, provinces, and cities
they cry out to their people in frenzy for deeds
so that masks of frustrations
and discontent due to hunger and lack of work
do not exhaust the minds of the workers with
irreversible actions of violence and fear.

And only parental love
that springs from the azure blue
escape to the surface
to calm the enraged fists.

Strange

One morning, I saw him arrive—attentive, jovial.
I saw him arrive one morning
but with an absent look of feeling toward me.
I greeted him; he greeted me.
He smiled at me; I smiled at him.
But still in his gaze, an absent feeling.
I saw no intention of affection toward me;
I kept waiting,
eager, eager for his hands to hold me
and wrap around my waist like they used to in decades
to feel his body adjusted to mine, his breath…
But it did not happen.
And again I observed him absent but kind.
Without losing his charisma, he spoke eloquently,
and I understood
that he was just my friend.
I had gotten my best friend back,
but I had lost my great love.
His gaze was clearly continuing,
absent of love for me.
And inside of me,
a broken feeling,
a spill, a failed encounter
in this longed-for meeting of passion
burning in me.
But you, a strange and absent feeling
in your eyes.

Fluids

Rain falling from the sky and hitting structures
And slides down its walls, impacting the ground.

Dirty water that runs in sewers
torrential water falling by gravity
from a powerful waterfall.

Tears that roll down your cheeks
of a woman who cries
because she has lost a loved one.

Cold, hot, or temperate liquid
what goes down our throat
refreshing us and quenching our thirst.

Thrombi circulating in the blood
of sclerotic arteries.

Powerful black liquid, called petroleum
that gushes out from within
from the ground up
defying all gravity.

Fluids, liquids
that make me reflect
about how special they are to life
even when we laugh, cry, work
or we serve the country.

Fires

Melted fire and pollution
the reddish sun complains
from the excessive heat that suffocates it.
And you can hardly see an occasional white cloud
stained by the fire
that burns excessively
out of control
devastating and devouring everything on its way.

The scenery of extensive vegetation
fears because it knows
that they can't stop the giant flames of fire
that attack aggressively.
And the structures of buildings and businesses
as well as some vehicles
which have nowhere to run
and they are consumed
by the ravenous flames.
The afternoon seemed almost night.
It seems to get old
by the mistreatment of the burning fire and its flames.

Giants

I know of giants who want to bring down trees
with his hands,
but they can't even
intimidate its branches
because they are so small
in purposes and ideas.

I know of giants that threaten
for its size,
but yet, far from intimidating,
they provoke the laughter from the little ones.
Those giants
who, enraged,
look down, defying
people without social status,
people with disoriented sexuality,
without regulation, without protection, without a defined
     God.
Those giants, I've seen them crumble
in his own colony,
leaving a black smoke of stupor,
and vanish to start a new opportunity
to a new definite and true tomorrow.

Heritage

My son,
we leave you an inheritance
of values, beliefs, independence, principles,
determination, responsibility, honesty,
dedication, compassion, firmness...
The solid experience that
always your parents
were there for you
whenever you needed it
with your prayers, your advice, your presence or not,
we were always close.

Inheritance of a million words of love,
of hundreds of acres of fortress,
of huge sows of confidence in yourself,
and valuable words of support and assurance.

There are inheritances of diseases,
of syndromes, bad habits, poverty, dysfunction,
alcoholism, violence...
Inheritance of taboos, of limitations,
also inheritance of good life.

Maybe we didn't have expensive jewelry
and properties to leave you
as an inheritance, but it was more valuable
what you inherited in yourself
as a human being,

those qualities that you possess
that make you shine and succeed
and achieve your purposes.
We consider you to be lucky.
And so your future generations will be.

Siblings

Like the fingers of the hand
we have been five siblings
united, loving
who support each other
and that, once, like the fingers of the hand
one supports the other to be able to retain
the trophy of life
for which it is needed
solidarity, patience, understanding
and much conviction of the love of God.

Like the five fingers of the hand
we have retained the course of life
with paper and pencil
with mechanical tools
botany and science
and finished our studies
of knowledge, which has led us
to establish our lives, our families
our destinies, to reap fruits
of that valuable unit
that is called brotherhood
and it is composed
of the five fingers of the hand.
Just like us five siblings
that make their parents proud
and their offspring.

Tears of the Heart

Tears flow from my heart;
my eyes are dry, thirsty, and cracked;
my troubled thoughts
of pain and anguish.
Tears flow from my heart;
it is impossible to think, act…
My hands are paralyzed;
my restless legs, today, are asleep.

Tears flow from my heart;
I can still hear laughter and conversations
from two, three decades ago,
good moments, divine moments of fullness.
But I'm still, motionless.

Tears flow from my heart;
I miss her little hands around my neck,
the brightness of his eyes
that were only for me,
the splendor of his perfect little face
at his young age,
his love, his smile, his trust
that gave life to my heart
that today tears of pain flow.

Hands Extended

Powerful contact we make
through them: the hands,
Hands to offer help to others.
With the hands, when shaking them to others,
we express pleasure, sincerity, respect, courtesy...
Hands to mold with art,
the Plasticine, the clay...
and create a star figure.
Hands for drawing on paper, canvas, or on the wall,
an artistic graphic.
Hands to hug and caress the cheek of your partner.
Hands to prescribe a food or medical prescription
to heal the sick who needs care.
Hands to write a book.
Strong hands of fieldworkers, construction,
or chain production.
Hands to do magic.
Hands to steal valuable items.
Hands to be read by people who practice palmistry.
Hands to point to the accused
and cry out for justice.
Hands to pray and be raised in petition.
Hands for playing sports or playing a musical instrument.
Hands to handle a team, a train, an airplane, or a vehicle.
Hands for the keyboard of a computer or a piano.
Hands to practice martial arts or to shoot a weapon.
Hands to hold the trophy of triumph or your child's hand.
Hands to applaud a good play or a successful singer
after its debut.
Hands to translate the language of silence.

Hands to direct traffic.
Hands to decorate dresses, walls, or cakes.
Strong hands, big, small, yellow, white, black,
delicate, deformed, dirty…but
that come together with a solid idea and a single voice…
Unity.

Looking at the Ground

From distant lands
I observe the impotence
and the pain of mine
before the groaning of the earth
shaking between brittle walls
debris, dirt
political and material obstacles
that are being cleaned
with tears from a sad cloudy sky

On earth
on the way, there are trapped
many belongings
mixed with discontent, fear, doubts…
that dissipate with frustration
and arms of different colors
trying to rescue hope.

Looking at the ground
green and reddish
hurt by the nature of time
hurt by the circumstances
mistreated and bullied
by their rulers and tyrants
that do not account for
the precious value of its people
brave and passionate for their land
who fight for their values
and for a better tomorrow.

Ship of Reflections

Who, like you, who flies overhead
oceans, cities, elevations, crops
that, with your wings, you gradually ascend and descend
to see with those windshield lenses
the perfection of creation,
the symmetry of the fields, the suspension of the clouds,
the wonderful colors of the earth
contrasting with the color of the vegetation,
experiencing a sense of heroic harmony
when you know you have control of your ship
to enjoy with pleasure from near or far
each and every one of the details that make up the universe.

Who, like you, what you plan day after day
perform this same act with new appearances
and experiences, who has seen the dawn,
the evening, and the dusk of the days.

Who, like you, who is polishing and adding hours,
longing for many to see the day and night from the height,
in a ship of reflections
to cherish with passion the next day that is about to happen.

—Dedicated to my son the pilot

Black

Black, the blackboard.
Black, oil.
Black, coal.
Black is my color.
Black, the margin of the notebook.
Black, the ink of my pen.
Blacks, my eyes.
Black, your hair.
Black, the magician's hat.
Blacks, the beans.
Black, the phone.
Black, my shoes.
Black, your car.
Black, the cat.
Black, the dog.
Black, the bat.
Black, the gorilla.
Black, a minority of the population.
Black, a defined and distinguished color.
Black, the color of my skin,
of which I am proud,
crying out for equal rights.

Ears

Ear canal and
component structure
of the five senses
through which the sound passes.

Ears, to listen
praises from my husband
that speak of the love he has for me.

Ears, to listen
your breath close to me.
Ears, to hear thrilling noises
of explosions, landslides, catastrophes…
Ears that betray terrifying rumors
of false friends.

Ears, to hear the song of a bird
and the melody of a beautiful love song.
Ears that hear encouragement, fervent prayer
motivation, a laugh, a cry, a lightning bolt, or silence.

Eyes

Eyes with a haughty look,
sad eyes,
black, green, and blue eyes,
envious eyes,
big, malicious eyes.
Eyes like lanterns
that illuminate the child's face before a new toy.
Eyes with a warm look
for the adored wife who just got off the bus
and is hugged by her husband
that waits for her impatiently.
Eyes to look at the criminal
that will be sentenced in a short time.
Heartbreaking eyes
because she mourns the loss of her child, her parents, or her
    spouse.
Slanted or round eyes.
Eyes to look at
poverty or wealth,
comedy or drama,
the sea and the sky,
the country or the city.
Eyes of tenderness
to appreciate the little creature which has just been born.
Eyes of rebellion or hatred.
Loving eyes.
Eyes of pity,
eyes of revenge,
eyes of pleasure,
of gratitude, of fatigue, of insecurity.

Puffy, irritated eyes.
Blind eyes.
Eyes that represent the light of the body
where a meal is accepted or rejected
a friendship or a proposition.
Illuminated or bright eyes
when answered to an all-powerful guidance.
Inert eyes
who look beyond
because they have gone to rest.
Multiple eyes.

Precise Instant

In that instant where the sunset gets dark,
in that instant where hope is defined,
of disappointment, in that instant where tears fall,
and the uncertainty ceases, in which your heart stops beating,
your eyes shine, your lips dry,
and your hands lose strength.

At that moment, you would say:
"Farewell me to the sun and the wheat."
Say goodbye to the sea,
say goodbye to paved roads, to life,
say goodbye to your love, to your kisses,
say goodbye to you, dear…
At that precise instant.

What Were We? What Are We?

What we were?
We were two children full of love, illusions, desires,
With a long list of dreams.
We were a happy, fulfilled couple with a home, with a child…
It was us! We were!
With ups and downs
With joys and sorrows,
With stumbles, erotic fantasies, with miracles, with visions;
With achievements and failures.
But always together in our prayers.

What are we?
You dust, and I matter.
You a memory; me a present.
Two lovers full of love separated by two dimensions.
You in heaven; me on earth.
You looking at your absence, and I am suffering it.
Me living a nightmare, and you in paradise.
That's what we are! We are that!
But still together in our prayers.

Tattoo

My love, you are not gone! I still breathe your sweat.
My eyes remain awake, and your gaze on me.
My lips wet by yours, flavored with you.
Penetrating is your laugh, your voice in my ears,
challenging my memory.
My hands still intertwined in yours,
tightly tight.
And you there, tattooed on me,
despite the passing time.

Storm

It rains outside torrentially.
It rains outside, and inside of me,
there is a storm.
Tears rain down my cheeks
with flashes of sobs.
And they seem not to stop.

Then comes the calm and winds of thoughts,
of melancholy and longing.
Like gusts
go through my mind,
they seem not to cease.

And looking for an end to this bad time,
with shell umbrellas,
I stop the rain of tears,
for the rainbow to appear
and make my face shine,
announcing that there will be no more storm,
that the bad weather has stopped,
and that spring days will come.

You Give Me

With the tenderness of a husband, you look at me
as if you wanted to retain each of my features in your mind.
You smile at me, giving me confidence
that the whole world belongs to both of us.
And in the same way
you give me love
you kiss me
you smell me
you take care of me
you pamper me
you adore me
you please me
you watch me
you claim me
you surrender, leaving no other option for me
but to love you and give all myself to you.

Only Reason

Reason to raise the wineglass
and toast to my story.
Reason to look
through the windshield of my car, people, fields, structures
and forget my present.
Reason to observe the universe with glasses
and fly with my imagination to a specific place.
Reason to open my bedroom window
and escape with just a glance into space.
Reason to see the photo of my only child
and know that I will always have his love, attention, his look
Reason to distinguish between defiance and reasoning
of dysfunctional or exceptional minds.
Reason to raise my hands and speak to my Creator
and, when lowering them, feel new energy throughout my
        body,
awakening in me love, trust, stability
Reason to write
this book of poetry and release toxins,
anxiety, and depression.
Only reason and reasons
to give thanks for everyday things,
the absurd, the logical.

To See You

Unpredictable, is that I see you again.
Erratic, keep thinking about our love.
Absurd, let me hear your voice again.
Confused, it's my way of thinking about a future with you.
Extraordinary, it is remembering our lives together.
Satisfactory, it was the time we shared
during all these years.
Admirable, that you saw what we managed
to do of our son and his achievements.
Unforgettable, the love that we lived
and what we promised ourselves in life, and we fulfilled
what we both were able to grow and mature.
Unattainable, were the days that we had to live
and the love that we lacked to give ourselves,
the wonders that together we would have known,
and the miracles that we would have conceived
if fate had given us more time.
Grateful, for all that was possible to achieve,
thanks to this love and what we build,
even with our mistakes.

Vicissitudes

A new year
has arrived;
something so desired
for the cure of the virus,
waiting for a turn
three hundred and sixty degrees.
Doing a brief recount
of this two thousand and twenty.
I'll tell you…what haven't we seen?
From acts of violence, erupting volcanoes,
cyclones, fires, pandemics…
People, I'm not lying to you;
they have left this world unexpectedly
to leave with the Lord.
Staying at home,
only pain and an immense emptiness
amid unemployment
and lack of food.
Optimism or disappointment,
there are two determinations
that we should take.
Follow the recommendations
of the experts:
get vaccinated,
do not crowd.
And fighting all together,
in that way, cooperating,
we will all go together,

every grain of sand,
until leaving everything behind
like a nightmare
and look at a new year
that shines
with health, more jobs, and unity.
It really seems
that God is angry
because His people do not obey.
We must create awareness;
let's leave the indulgences
that lead to nothing.
Let us bow down to Him
following the guidelines,
growing in faith and love
at His call,
being forgiven
how many fouls we make.
And rest assured, we will be
a better-formed people!
My friends,
God is love,
and He wants a better future.
Let's walk safe please;
that this new year,
it will be prosperous and supportive.
Nothing else
to confirm.
Kneel and humble ourselves before HIM,
and we will see a solution
to all our dilemmas.

With triumph and satisfaction,
we will have a better tomorrow.
We will open doors, windows,
airports, and borders
without looking at the barriers
that used to limit us.

About the Author

Regla Teresa Dominguez was born in the city of Santa Clara, Cuba, on September 20, 1960. Daughter of Gelacio Alberto Dominguez and Agustina Teresa Prieto, she grew up in a family of four male siblings: Ángel, Mario, Gerardo, and Gelacio. She exercised a career in dentistry in his native country for ten years.

From her twenty-eight-year marriage to Carlos Martín Rodriguez, she had only one son, Carlos Alberto Rodríguez Dominguez.

In 1993, she settled in the USA, where she lives in the city of Los Angeles, California.

Her poems are focused on the family, what she appreciates. They are a tribute to her husband, to the love they had and professed for their son.

The poetry book *Feelings* makes public her vocation as a writer for the first time with an unpublished work cultivated for years but without coming to light.

CPSIA information can be obtained
at www.ICGtesting.com
Printed in the USA
LVHW101950060622
720619LV00004B/710